GETTING TO KNOW
THE U.S. PRESIDENTS

WILLIAM HENRY
HARRISON

NINTH PRESIDENT
1841

WRITTEN AND ILLUSTRATED BY MIKE VENEZIA

CHILDREN'S PRESS®
A DIVISION OF SCHOLASTIC INC.
NEW YORK   TORONTO   LONDON   AUCKLAND   SYDNEY
MEXICO CITY   NEW DELHI   HONG KONG
DANBURY, CONNECTICUT

Reading Consultant: Nanci R. Vargus, Ed.D., Assistant Professor, School of Education, University of Indianapolis

Historical Consultant: Marc J. Selverstone, Ph.D., Assistant Professor, Miller Center of Public Affairs, University of Virginia

Photographs © 2005: Art Resource, NY: 22 (National Portrait Gallery, Smithsonian Institution, Washington, D.C.), 15 (Smithsonian American Art Museum, Washington, D.C.); Bridgeman Art Library International Ltd., London/New York: 9 (Chateau de Versailles, France/Lauros/Giraudon), 8 (Delaware Art Museum, Wilmington, DE, USA/Howard Pyle Collection), 25 (Delaware Art Museum, Wilmington, DE, USA/Louisa DuPont Copeland Memorial Fund), 27 (New-York Historical Society, New York, USA); Brown Brothers: 20; Corbis Images/Bettmann: 3, 6 bottom; Hulton|Archive/Getty Images: 17; Library of Congress, Prints and Photographs Division: 19, 29, 32; North Wind Picture Archives: 14; Ohio Historical Society: 18; PictureHistory.com: 31; Stock Montage, Inc.: 13; Superstock, Inc.: 6 top (The Huntington Library, Art Collections, and Botanical Gardens, San Marino, CA); The Image Works/EANA: 30; University of Pennslyvania Archives: 11.

Colorist for illustrations: Dave Ludwig

Library of Congress Cataloging-in-Publication Data

Venezia, Mike.
  William Henry Harrison / written and illustrated by Mike Venezia.
     p. cm. — (Getting to know the U.S. presidents)
  Includes bibliographical references and index.
  ISBN 0-516-22614-2 (lib. bdg.)   0-516-27483-X (pbk.)
  1. Harrison, William Henry, 1773-1841—Juvenile literature. 2.
Presidents—United States—Biography—Juvenile literature. I. Title.
  E392.V46 2004
  973.5'8'092—dc22

                                    2004000320

1 2 3 4 5 6 7 8 9 10 R 14 13 12 11 10 09 08 07 06 05

A portrait by Albert Gallatin Hoit of William Henry Harrison as president

William Henry Harrison was the ninth president of the United States. He was born on his family's plantation in Charles City County, Virginia, in 1773. No one ever got a chance to find out if William would have been a good president. That's because he served the shortest amount of time in office of any president in history.

On the day William Henry Harrison was sworn in as president, he decided to give a very long speech. It was a cold, wet, windy day. William was so excited that he didn't bother to wear a coat, hat, or gloves.

President Harrison caught a bad cold that soon turned into pneumonia. Only thirty-two days later, William Henry Harrison died in the White House. Vice President John Tyler took over the job as president of the United States.

A portrait of Benjamin Franklin by Joseph Siffred Duplessis (Huntington Library, Art Collections, and Botanical Gardens, San Marino, California)

When William Henry Harrison was born, Virginia was one of the thirteen colonies in North America ruled by Great Britain.

William was the youngest of seven children. Instead of going to school, he and his brother and sisters were schooled at home by a tutor. The Harrisons were pretty wealthy.

A portrait of George Washington by Charles Willson Peale

William's father was famous for being one of the signers of the Declaration of Independence. He also served as governor of Virginia. All kinds of interesting people would stop by William's home to visit his father, including Benjamin Franklin and George Washington.

The Battle of Yorktown, shown in this painting by Howard Pyle, occurred just a few miles from William Henry Harrison's boyhood home.

During this time, George Washington was commander-in-chief of the American army. The people of the thirteen colonies were fighting a war for freedom and independence from their rulers in Britain. William Henry Harrison was eight years old when the final battle of the Revolutionary War took place.

In 1781, General George Washington forced the British to surrender at the Battle of Yorktown, Virginia. Yorktown was just a few miles from the Harrisons' plantation. William probably saw hundreds of proud soldiers marching home from their victory.

A painting showing General George Washington (in blue coat with gold vest) at the Battle of Yorktown, by Louis Charles Auguste Couder (Chateau de Versailles, France)

As a young boy, William was always willing to help out anyone who had a cut, sprain, or injury. Mr. and Mrs. Harrison thought it might be a good idea if their son became a doctor.

William ended up attending some of the best medical schools in the country, including the University of Pennsylvania in Philadelphia. While he was in medical school, his father died unexpectedly. As soon as William got over the shock, he began to change his mind about his career.

An engraving showing the University of Pennsylvania in the late 1700s

William Henry Harrison learned about a huge area of land west of Pennsylvania called the Northwest Territory. This territory would later become what is now the midwestern region of the United States. People from all over the original colonies were traveling there in hopes of finding a better life. William imagined finding a better life there, too. He felt the best way to start his adventure would be to join the army. In 1791, at the age of eighteen, William Henry Harrison enlisted in the United States Army.

A map of the
Northwest
Territory in
1787

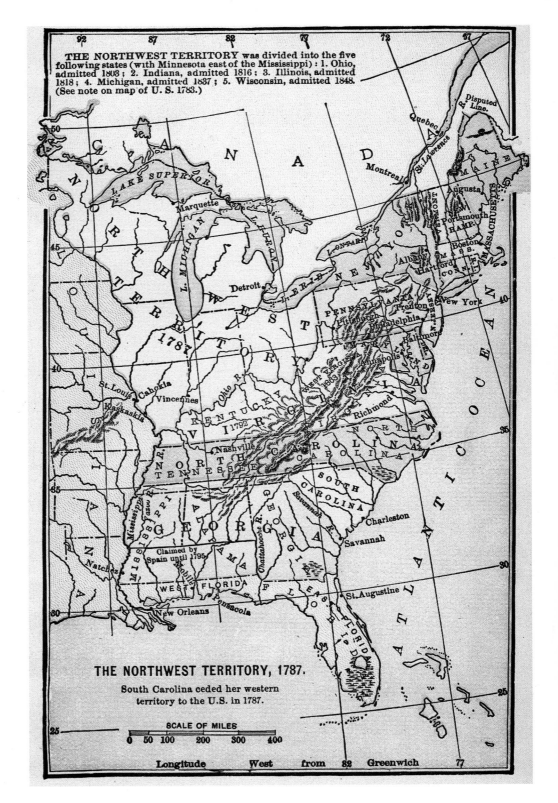

THE NORTHWEST TERRITORY was divided into the five following states (with Minnesota east of the Mississippi): 1. Ohio, admitted 1803; 2. Indiana, admitted 1816; 3. Illinois, admitted 1818; 4. Michigan, admitted 1837; 5. Wisconsin, admitted 1848. (See note on map of U. S. 1783.)

THE NORTHWEST TERRITORY, 1787.

South Carolina ceded her western
territory to the U.S. in 1787.

SCALE OF MILES

0   50 100   200   300   400

Longitude   West   from   82 Greenwich   77

A settler's cabin in the Northwest Territory in the early 1800s

Soldiers were badly needed in the Northwest Territory to protect settlers from angry American Indians. Many American Indian peoples were trying to keep white settlers out of the Northwest Territory. The Indians had been there first, and they felt the land was theirs to be used for hunting, fishing, and trapping.

Most Indian leaders wanted their people to live as they had for thousands of years. Unfortunately, the United States government didn't care very much about the feelings and opinions of American Indians.

A painting showing Sauk and Fox Indians along a river in the Northwest Territory

The thousands of settlers who were moving west wanted to set up forts, trading posts, homes, farms, and businesses. Some tribal leaders were tempted by offers of money and agreed to sell their land to the U.S. government, but many refused. Bloody battles often broke out between American Indians and settlers or U.S. soldiers.

A portrait of Tecumseh

Soon after William Henry Harrison joined the army, he traveled down the Ohio River to Fort Washington, which is today part of Cincinnati, Ohio. Harrison arrived there right after a fierce battle had taken place. The U.S. Army didn't do very well in the battle. William learned that one of the leaders of the Indians was a great Shawnee warrior named Tecumseh. William Henry Harrison would meet Tecumseh often throughout his career.

A painting showing the 1794 Battle of Fallen Timbers

William Henry Harrison turned out to be an excellent soldier. He was smart and fought bravely. William was quickly promoted to higher ranks until he became a captain. He was then put in charge of Fort Washington.

William helped win the important Battle of
Fallen Timbers, which forced most American
Indians out of the region. Now it was safer for
even more settlers to move into the Fort
Washington area.

William Henry Harrison was made commander of Fort Washington (above) in 1795.

Anna Symmes Harrison

When Judge John Symmes and his family
moved to the Fort Washington area, William
Henry Harrison met Anna Symmes, the
judge's daughter. Anna and William soon fell
in love and decided to get married. Judge
Symmes disapproved of the marriage, though.

He thought that a soldier couldn't make enough money to support his daughter and that a soldier's life was too dangerous.

One day, when Judge Symmes was out of town on a business trip, William and Anna went ahead and got married without the judge's approval.

A portrait by Rembrandt Peale of William Henry Harrison in military dress (National Portrait Gallery, Smithsonian Institution, Washington, D.C.)

Eventually, William Henry Harrison decided to leave the army. He was interested in seeing if there were other ways to make a living and raise a family in the Northwest Territory. William and Anna ended up having ten children.

Over the next few years, William Henry's career really took off. In 1800, President John Adams asked him to govern a huge part of the Northwest Territory called the Indiana Territory. This region included most of what is today Indiana, Illinois, Michigan, Minnesota, and Wisconsin.

Harrison's main problem became Tecumseh. Tecumseh was busy trying to unite the Chickasaw, Choctaw, Miami, and Creek Indians to join him in raids against the settlers.

As more and more settlers moved into the Indiana Territory, the U.S. government did everything it could to get American Indians to sell their land. It often tricked Indians into giving their land away for almost nothing. Tecumseh was really angry now. He and his warriors attacked even more settlements.

In 1810, Tecumseh went to William Henry Harrison's home in Indiana to warn him that if the American government took any more land from the Indians, it would mean war.

Over a period of fifteen years, William Henry Harrison convinced more American Indians to sell their land. He also worked hard trying to stop Tecumseh and his warriors from killing settlers. William even held peace talks at his home with Tecumseh, but they could never agree on anything.

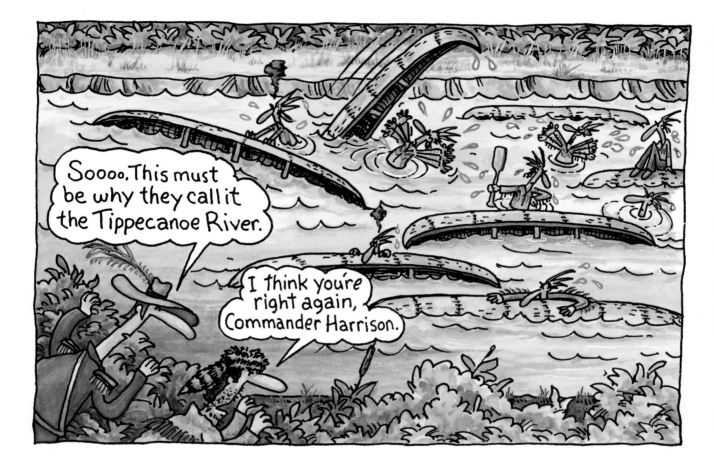

As powerful and clever a leader as Tecumseh was, William Henry Harrison still managed to win the most important battles against him. Once, when Tecumseh was off trying to gather more warriors, William Henry Harrison gathered his own troops.

He led them to an important Indian settlement called Prophetstown. It was by the Tippecanoe River near what is today Lafayette, Indiana. On November 7, 1811, a huge battle broke out. William Henry Harrison led his soldiers to victory and burned Prophetstown to the ground.

A painting showing the Battle of Tippecanoe

The Battle of Tippecanoe made William Henry Harrison famous all across the United States. When the nation's second war with Great Britain began in 1812, William Henry was made a major general.

Even though the United States had won its independence from England years earlier, many British still wanted to get some of the country back. General Harrison was asked to stop the British from helping Tecumseh and his warriors fight against the United States.

General Harrison's soldiers chased the British out of the Northwest Territory into Canada. During a battle near the Thames River, the great leader Tecumseh was killed.

Tecumseh was killed by Harrison's forces during the 1813 Battle of the Thames River.

The Battle at Thames River made General Harrison even more famous. In 1814, he headed home to his family in Ohio. Over the next few years, he spent a lot of time trying to get elected to government jobs. He served in Congress, first as a U.S. representative and later as a U.S. senator.

A Whig Party rally for Harrison during the presidential election of 1840

In 1836, a new political group thought William Henry Harrison might make a good president. This group was called the Whig Party. They convinced William Henry to run as one of the three candidates they were supporting for president.

William Henry lost his first presidential race to Martin Van Buren, but he easily won the next election, in 1840. This time, the Whigs went all out to get voters interested in him. They threw parties, gave away gifts, and printed posters with catchy slogans.

One of the best slogans was "Tippecanoe and Tyler, too!" Tippecanoe was a nickname given to William Henry Harrison. Tyler was John Tyler, who was running with Harrison for vice president. William spent time traveling around the country giving speeches about himself.

Soon after he won the election, President Harrison gave his very long inaugural speech in the cold, wet weather. He died exactly one month later, on April 4, 1841.

William Henry Harrison was sworn in as president on March 4, 1841.

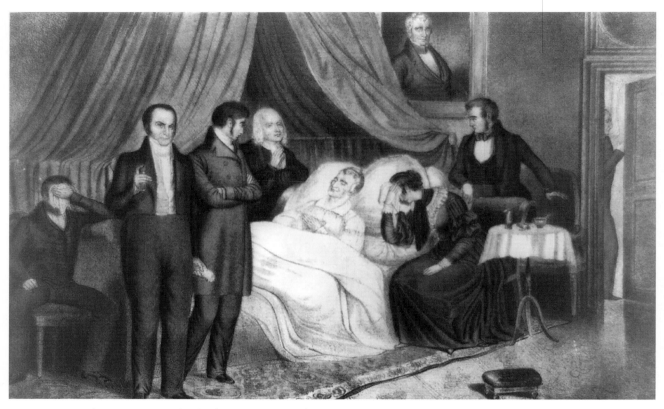
President Harrison died of pneumonia after only thirty-two days in office.

William Henry Harrison didn't have time to do much at all as president. He is best remembered for being a successful military leader, for the exciting political campaign he and his supporters created—and, of course, for being the first president to die in office.